MW00448253

The End of

Codependency

*How to Stop Controlling and Enabling Others,
Love Yourself, Have Happy Relationships,
and be Codependent No More*

By: Laura Raskin

The End of Codependency

The End of Codependency

Legal notice

This book is copyright (c) 2016 by Laura Raskin. All rights reserved. This book may not be copied or duplicated in whole or in part via any means including electronic forms of duplication such as audio or video recording or transcription. The contents of this book may not be stored in any retrieval system, transmitted, or otherwise copied for any use whether public or private, other than brief quotations contained in articles or reviews which fall under the "fair use" exception, without express prior permission of the publisher.

This book provides information only. The reader accepts all responsibility for how he or she chooses to use the information contained in this book and under no circumstances will the author or publisher be held liable for any damages caused directly or indirectly by any information contained in this book.

The End of Codependency

Introduction

Do you wish you could spend every waking hour with your partner? Do you get jealous when they're with other people, and are afraid that you would lose your "better half" if they left? Do you have a history of struggling with low self-esteem, a vague sense of your identity, and an inability to really pinpoint what you want in life?

If you answered yes to any of these three questions, then you have codependent tendencies. The term "codependency" originally applied mostly to the partners of addicts, but now it applies to anyone who has trouble taking care of their own needs and instead focuses nearly exclusively on their significant other. People can be codependent in friendships and at work, as well, and we will get into that a little in this book, but it's mostly about how codependency plays out in romantic relationships.

In this book, you'll learn what codependency is and how it is actually often idolized in the media as being a defining and necessary quality of a passionate romance, while in reality, it destroys relationships. You'll also learn about how codependency begins and that how you were raised plays a major role in whether or not you are a codependent adult. Abuse, neglect, and other dysfunctions within families all affect the identity you grew into. The main body of this book thoroughly explores the four types of codependents: the Martyr, Savior, Coach, and People-pleaser. Many codependents display a mix of traits associated with these types, and often are all four at once. Breaking the types into sections allows us to take a closer look at specific tendencies, as well as specific solutions.

As you read, you might realize that your partner is the codependent one, or maybe you *both* are. Learning how to respond to codependency instead of trying to "fix" the other person is really the only good reaction, so that chapter will cover ways to behave according to each type of codependent. The final chapter will describe what a healthy relationship should look like.

Everyone deserves to be happy and deserves to know who they are outside of their relationship with their significant other. When a person truly believes they are valuable and lovable, life will be so much better than it was before. Relationships will grow and thrive. It's time to put codependency in the past and embrace what love is meant to be.

Chapter 1: What Is Codependency?

The term "codependency" originally applied just to people in relationships with drug and/or alcohol addicts, and the behaviors that enabled addictions. Experts and therapists who were treating alcoholics and drug addicts realized that those in relationships with the addict played a major role in the problem. While their partners believed they were helping their addicted significant other, they were actually making recovery harder and not allowing the addict to become more independent. Treatment began to include the partner, so they could learn how to help their loved one without enabling them.

As time went on, the definition of "codependent" broadened, so it's no longer exclusive to the partners of addicts. It describes any relationship where the codependent constantly sacrifices their own needs for their partner. Instead of enabling a chemical addiction, the codependent enables emotional immaturity, irresponsibility, chronic insecurity, untreated mental illness, abuse, and so on.

Emotional codependency makes a person feel like they are nothing without their partner. They have such low self-esteem, they are willing to put up with all kinds of terrible behavior just so they don't lose that person. Putting up with bad behavior enables it, and in order for life to work, a codependent has to pick up the slack. They take on the role of a caregiver, savior, what have you; the codependent's identity is totally wrapped up in how they serve or "save" their partner. They aren't happy with their life, but they don't know who they would be if they left.

This sense of responsibility for a partner's behavior often results in the need to control everything, because the codependent's sense of worth is tied up in what and how their partner is doing. When their partner is sad, the codependent is sad. In order to feel happy again, the codependent tries to change their partner's mood, not their own. Their partner is the most important thing.

The End of Codependency

Women Trained To Be Codependent

Everyone has the potential to be codependent, but it's worth mentioning how codependency in women has actually been encouraged in the past. The old-fashioned, misogynist view of a "good woman" was one who put others before herself, took responsibility for the home and children, and always deferred to what her husband wanted. Though times have changed in many ways, women are still fighting the battle for self-esteem and approval from men. Women are constantly lectured on how they should look and behave. Even seemingly well-intentioned articles like, "Clothing Styles That Men Hate," "10 Things A Lady Should Never Do In Public," and "Reasons Why Men Prefer Natural Beauty" are sending the message that a woman needs to present herself in a way that's acceptable for men.

Men, in turn, are often taught that their voices matter the most, and that a girl who makes good "wife material" is one who will always listen to what they say. "Bossy" girls are unappealing. Women who make more money are also off the table for a lot of guys. Men like this treat women poorly, with little respect, and women who have been raised with low self-esteem are drawn towards those men. Even when relationships between these two types of people results in unhappiness, history repeats itself. Bad habits are hard to break.

As mentioned earlier, men can be codependent, too. It's not as if women are at an "increased risk," necessarily, just because of their sex. It's just that for many years, codependency in women was idealized, so codependent women might face less resistance to their tendencies. They might even be praised for their good ol'-fashioned values. The rest of this book is neutral in terms of gender unless mentioned otherwise.

The End of Codependency

Codependency Idolized In Media

In movies, TV, and books, codependent relationships are often still considered extremely romantic. The "Twilight" series of books and movies features a submissive heroine, Bella, who is completely undefined except for her relationship to her vampire lover Edward. In "The Notebook," Noah's life comes to a screeching halt when he's separated from Allie and he says things like, "Just tell me what you want be to be, and I'll be that for you." Even in movies for kids, like "The Little Mermaid," characters frequently go to dramatic, even dangerous lengths to be with the person they love, ignoring concerns from family and friends. A quick Google image search of "romantic love quotes" brings up troubling phrases like "Without you, I'm nothing," "Losing you is my worst fear," and "Sometimes I can't see myself when I'm with you, I only see you." Clearly, many people have a warped idea of what true love should be like.

While a lot of codependent relationships in the media are not portrayed as totally positive or healthy, the whole "I can't breathe without you" mentality is still depicted as epic and romantic. People want passion in their lives, and too often, codependency is offered up as a relationship goal.

The End of Codependency

What Codependency Does To People

When a person is codependent, what happens? What does life look like? Codependent people live a hectic, anxiety-ridden existence with their partner. It's easy to start feeling resentful. Resentment and bitterness is poison to any relationship. When the codependent harbors bitterness against their partner, they're usually unable to take any action. They feel unappreciated, but don't actually want to give up their duties, because that means they lose their role and sense of worth. They just keep shoving their own desires deep down and grinding on. This prevents any positive change, and the relationship just keeps circling back around to the same problems. No one learns and no one grows in a relationship like that.

Living in a state of constant insecurity is bad for a person's health. Because codependents constantly need validation from others, especially their loved one, they're *always* insecure. This can lead to depression, clinical anxiety, and dramatic mood swings. The mental state always has an effect on the physical body, so a codependent person might also experience stomach problems, severe headaches, high blood pressure, exhaustion, and insomnia. Due to codependents having trouble taking care of themselves, like taking the time to go to a doctor, these physical ailments can become severe. To cope, they might take to popping anti-anxiety pills or testing out other solutions that don't actually address the real problem.

So, we have a better idea of what codependency is and the consequences of that kind of relationship, but where does codependency come from? It can't be something that just appears as soon as a person enters a romantic relationship. There has to be early signs and other influences in a person's life. The next chapter will get into where all of this starts and how codependent habits form.

The End of Codependency

15

Chapter 2: The Roots of Codependency

Like most personal issues, codependency starts as a result of how a person was raised. Even if their childhood wasn't great, people tend to reenact their family dynamic in their adult relationships. This explains why abuse victims frequently abuse their own children, and why alcoholics usually have other alcoholics in their family. Recent studies have even shown that trauma can be carried on through DNA, affecting how a person handles grief and other crises. It's no surprise that a person's upbringing is going to affect how they function in every relationship.

Children either get too much attention, too little attention, or somewhere in the middle. Those who have the highest risk of becoming codependent adults are usually part of families with at least one of these dysfunctions: abuse, neglect, or addiction/illness.

The End of Codependency

Childhoods With Abuse

In families where there's abuse (emotional, sexual, etc), children are unable to develop good self-esteem. The person inflicting the abuse teaches the child that their needs and boundaries don't matter, and that they are just there to meet the abuser's wants. Even if the child isn't the one being abused (it's a sibling, mother, other family member), the child witnesses a broken family dynamic. They see how powerless the abused person is and how the abuser disrespects an individual's personhood at every turn. Instead of living in a nurturing environment, the child lives in a toxic one that stunts their emotional maturity. The child isn't able to come into their own as an independent person. There's a lot of fear and anxiety associated with their loved ones, so when they grow up, that's what they are drawn towards.

A lot of people are confused about why victims of abuse always seem to end up with another abuser, which unfortunately leads to disdain instead of understanding. People believe the abuse can't possibly be "that bad" if the person stays with their partner, or that somehow the abused person must "deserve" the abuse.

Beliefs like this reveal a fundamental ignorance about how abused people function. Abused people often don't know

17

what healthy relationships are, and are naturally drawn towards what they know. They *expect* a relationship to have an abnormal amount of fear, and until they are able to get therapy and see that they do deserve better, they'll keep dismissing abuse and pushing aside their own needs. There's also a heavy cloud of fear in abusive relationships; the idea of leaving is often more dangerous than staying.

The End of Codependency

Childhoods With Neglect

When people were raised in neglectful families, they can become very clingy and needy as adults. When they were young, they were isolated and lonely, and grew up craving love. As adults, they'll do just about anything to get and keep the attention of their loved one, even if it means not doing what's best for themselves or the relationship as a whole. This could include always doing what the other person wants, letting their partner develop destructive behaviors, or ignoring their own needs for fear that their partner will be unhappy with them.

As children, they weren't given unconditional love, but were taught that they had to earn it. They always had to do something or be a certain way to get noticed. They always had to be the perfect child, the straight-A student, the sports star, and so on. They associated success and fulfilling a certain role with their parents' attention and love. This habit will follow them into adulthood and they'll jump into relationships eager to please, so they can always have someone with them.

These codependents need attention to feel happy and valued. When their partner is busy with something else, the codependent isn't secure enough to believe their partner still loves them. If their partner doesn't pay enough

19

attention to them or give the "right" kind of attention, the codependent will become depressed and resentful. However, they are usually too afraid to confront their loved one for fear it will push them away, so those negative emotions build up and ruin the relationship.

Childhoods With Addiction/Illness

Kids who come from families with addiction or illness are often used to playing the role of a caregiver and/or martyr. With all the attention focused on the family member with the addiction or illness, the child has to put aside their own needs and/or spend all their time and energy helping to care for the family. They never really get to be taken care of, so they had to fend for themselves. Being so young, the techniques they picked up to deal with their emotions probably aren't going to work very well when they get older. There was no one there to show them better, so they just continue with their old habits.

Kids with addiction/illness-affected childhoods frequently become the caregivers, which is how they will see themselves as they grow up and enter new relationships. They'll baby their partner and take on all the work, neglecting good self-care. When they can't be the ones to take responsibility for everything, they lose their sense of purpose. Their brains tell them, "I need to take care of my partner in order to achieve their love. I don't know who I am if I'm not the one taking responsibility."

21

The End of Codependency

What If Your Childhood Was Normal?

You might be thinking, "My childhood didn't have any abuse, neglect, addiction, or illness! How could I be codependent?" Even if you had a great, healthy childhood with loving parents, there's still a chance you might be ingrained with some codependent tendencies. All of us, in one way or another, are raised to be codependent because all kids are codependent. When we're little, we look to our parents for everything, including our identity. As we age, we gradually break from our parents and form our own opinions, likes, dislikes, and so on. Our parents' reactions to this change affects if we see our individual selves as "good" or "bad."

Even healthy families tend to divide up children into different roles. A kid might be "the smart one" and feel like they've let their parents down if they get a poor grade on a test. If their parents don't counter that belief, a kid can grow up believing they have to always fit into the "smart" role in order to be loved. When they enter a romantic relationship, they'll need their partner to tell them they are smart, or they feel worthless. Their relationship with their partner will be like one with a boss, complete with evaluations on "how they're doing" and emotional promotions and raises.

The End of Codependency

Even just the number of siblings in a family can determine codependency. If you had a lot of siblings, your role in your family would be different than if you were an only child. With a lot of siblings, or even just one other sibling who required a lot of attention from your parents, you might have been neglected at times. If you came from a strict home with a lot of rules, you might have felt controlled, and will in turn feel the need to control everything when you grow up. If your family was religious, the "others before yourself" mentality might have been emphasized.

Does any of this sound familiar? Do you see where your childhood might have put you at risk for codependency? The next chapter will cover more specifics and questions to ask yourself, so you can find out.

Chapter 3: How Do You Know If You're Codependent?

The classic example of a codependent relationship is one where at least one of the people involved is an addict of some kind. Sometimes, both people are addicts and both are codependent. If you are with a current addict and/or have a history of being with addicts, you almost certainly have a codependent relationship. However, we know that not all codependent relationships involve addictive substances. Sometimes it's physical abuse or a severe mental illness that isn't under control, like bipolar disorder. Sometimes it isn't even necessarily "that bad," but you consistently ignore things that bother you because you're afraid you'll make your partner angry, and you'll lose them.

Even if you don't have a history of codependency, you can develop those traits if you start to neglect your interests, friends, and other aspects of your life in favor of your partner's. It can be a slow build until eventually, you have no life. This can happen if your partner has a stronger personality than you and asserts themselves more clearly. It becomes habit to just go along with what they want, so when problems arise, you've forgotten how to have good boundaries or let things go.

Here is a list of questions that can help you determine if you are in a codependent relationship:

- Do you spend all your time with your partner, or find yourself always thinking about them when you're apart?

- Do you ignore issues you have with your partner because you don't want to make them angry with you?

- Do other people say that you "baby" your partner too much and don't let them do things that adults should be able to do?

- Do you always do what your partner wants, even when you don't want to?

- Do you have trouble figuring out what you really want or feel?

If you answered yes to at least one of these questions, you probably have codependent tendencies. If you answered yes to multiple questions, you are most likely a codependent.

The End of Codependency

Codependency can look a bit different from person to person, but in general, there are four "types" of codependents: the Martyr, the Savior, the Coach, and the People-Pleaser. Oftentimes, a person can be all four at once.

The Martyr

A codependent who has a martyr complex is someone who believes suffering for love is the right thing to do. They'll make any sacrifice - even without being asked - because it makes them feel like a good person and good partner.

The Savior

A codependent playing the role of the savior or white knight wants to save or fix their partner. They're possessive and overprotective, and need to be their partner's business all the time.

The Coach

Because the codependent's sense of self is totally wrapped up in their partner, they take every success or failure personally. They are there to coach and instruct their partner's every move, because they don't trust their partner to do the right thing, or at least what the codependent wants.

The People-Pleaser

The End of Codependency

This codependent can't say no to anything. They just want to make their partner happy, so they will become whoever they think their partner wants them to be. This means squashing their own desires, interests, goals, etc.

Chapter 4: The Martyr

Let's dive deeper into what being a codependent with a martyr complex looks like. A Martyr blames their partner for how they feel and cannot take responsibility for the part they play in relationship problems. Instead of doing anything about the problems, the codependent hoards that pain, believing that's the right thing to do when you love someone. Sometimes that belief is not a conscious one, and the Martyr can't explain why they endure bad behavior. This could spring from a lack of self-esteem where the person needs to suffer for someone else in order to feel kind, compassionate, and good. Without that suffering, life has no meaning, and the person feels empty. That's why a Martyr can't leave the relationship.

Because a Martyr believes that the way to show love is to always put someone else's needs first, they often expect their partner to do the same for them. When they don't, resentment builds up, leading a codependent to criticize their partner for their behavior and say things like, "I do everything for you, and you don't appreciate me." If they don't complain directly to their partner, they'll talk to anyone who will listen. Friends and family will see the codependent as a "whiner." However, the Martyr won't

28

take any steps towards actually breaking out of the victim role, but will continue to cycle through suffering and complaining.

Here are some signs that you are playing the Martyr in your relationship:

- You feel like you make all the compromises and sacrifices in your relationship.

- You frequently volunteer to give up on your own dreams/desires in favor of your partner's, when they haven't asked you to.

- You're always complaining about your relationship to friends and family.

- You blame your partner's behavior for everything that's wrong in the relationship.

- You reject any outside advice about how to change *your* behavior.

- People frequently tell you, "You do too much for (*your partner's name*)."
- You are always painting yourself as the victim or someone for whom others should feel sorry.

29

The End of Codependency

Playing The Martyr In Friendships And Your Career

Friendships don't look too different from romantic relationships when it comes to martyrdom. You always drop everything for your friend whenever they have a problem or want to talk. You feel like the "good" one in the friendship, like you're doing something noble and brave by being friends with them. However, it feels like the friendship is one-sided and that your friend isn't investing as much into it as you are. That makes you resent them, and you frequently complain to other friends about them, but you can't end the friendship.

At work, you cast yourself in the role of the always-reliable worker. You stay late, take on extra projects, and don't make time for interests outside of work. When you get tired or overwhelmed, you often feel resentful towards colleagues who aren't putting in the work like you do. You feel unappreciated. At the same time, you don't like giving away work, because you believe you're the only one who is capable of doing it right.

How To Break Out Of The Martyr Role

If you believe you're playing the Martyr in your relationship, there's a way out. There are practical ways and also more thought-based ways to begin seeing yourself as a whole person who doesn't need to play the victim to feel valuable. Here are the practical ways to change:

- Begin to break bad communication (or lack of communication) habits like complaining to friends, sulking, never being available to talk to your partner, skirting hard topics with your partner, and so on.

- Think of actual actions you can take to address problems you have in your relationship instead of just stuffing down your emotions.

- Practice telling your partner how you feel about things in a way that isn't accusatory. For example, instead of saying, "You're so inconsiderate when you go out with your friends without telling me," try saying, "I feel neglected when you don't tell me when you're going out." This keeps the focus on *you* and your emotions.

31

- Take time to appreciate what you really love about your partner by giving them one compliment a day, and doing "couple" stuff like cuddling and going out at least once a week.

- Tell your partner that you want to go to couples' therapy, but ask in a way that doesn't blame them for the problems. One idea would be to say, "I've been feeling unhappy and want to work with a therapist on how we communicate."

The thought-based solutions are just as, if not more, necessary in order to rid yourself of the martyr complex. It takes the most work, but allows you to understand why you play the victim. A therapist that works alone with you would be extremely helpful, because they can ask you questions you might not have thought were important before.

- Think about *why* you always play the victim. Do you believe that you somehow deserve to be treated badly? Have you always been a martyr in your relationships?

- Begin to take responsibility for your own decisions instead of blaming your partner. You will start to see that you aren't doomed to feel pain because of your partner's decisions, but that you have control

over your emotions, and can make your own
decisions to achieve happiness.

- Assess the state of your relationship and if you need
  to think about leaving it behind. This is especially
  important if your partner is abusive.

- Work on putting your needs first, and then turning
  towards others. If you don't take care of yourself
  first, you can't give to others, because you're
  drawing from an empty well. This can be a really
  hard step depending on how you were raised,
  because many times people believe that putting
  themselves first is selfish.

Chapter 5: The Savior

Saviors need someone to save. The partners of Saviors are frequently people with serious problems like alcoholism or drug addiction. There's a clear "bad guy" that they need to be saved from, and the Savior wants to be the one to do it. The "bad guy" could also be a mental illness, a spiritual crisis, or even just something that the Savior doesn't like about their partner. Saviors are always looking for something to fix in their partner, because without a "bad guy" to deal with, the codependent feels like they have no purpose.

Unfortunately, the savior complex is often encouraged as a trait for men to adopt. "Good" men should want to be white knights and sweep in to save their partner from any and all harm. Even many religions teach that godly men need to both provide for and protect their partners; it's supposedly part of the male DNA. On the flip side, women are often taught that they need to "step back" and let men play into that hero fantasy. However, this complex doesn't work in real life and causes real problems.

Saviors are controlling and possessive of their partners, because they believe they have to shield them from all the

34

bad and harmful things in the world. When their partner starts to veer away from what the Savior thinks is best, it creates a lot of anxiety. The Savior is compelled to jump in and save the day, even when they haven't been asked. It gives them a sense of purpose. It can also cause resentment, though, when the Savior doesn't feel appreciated for all that they do.

On the other hand, when a Savior's partner is doing well and being independent, the Savior usually feels useless, and starts to look for things to fix. This can make their partner feel smothered, like they're married to an overbearing parent, and they'll start to push back. Of course, this gives the Savior even more anxiety, and they often become paranoid that their partner is finding their "white knight" elsewhere. Many times, the Savior starts to look for someone else to save, and becomes unfaithful. It's not uncommon for Saviors to have a long string of relationships where they left as soon as they felt useless.

Here are some key signs of having a savior complex:

- You always need to know where your partner is, who they're with, and what they're doing.

- You get jealous when your partner gets help from someone that's not you.

35

- You're always stepping in to take the reins from your partner, and often feel taken for granted.

- You feel a strong sense of duty towards your partner.

- You believe it's your job to "take care" of your partner.

- You feel good and strong when your partner comes to you for help or comfort.

- The best thing your partner can say to you is, "I need you."

Being The Savior In Friendships And Your Career

It's pretty rare for someone who is a Savior in their relationship to not play that same role in every area of their life. With their friends, the Savior is often just as protective as they are with their partner, and is known for hovering and wanting to know everything about their friends' lives. They're always the first ones to help with moving, rent money, babysitting, and anything else their friends might need. Saviors can become jealous of other friends, and frequently say things like, "So-and-so doesn't care about you as much as I do," and, "Why did you ask so-and-so for help? You should have asked me."

At work, Saviors are always taking on everyone else's jobs. If someone expresses a concern about something, the Savior is there to offer help. This can appear to be a good thing, because it looks like the Savior is being a strong team player, but the Savior doesn't know when to stop helping. This can cause them to fall behind in their own work, but to Saviors, it's worth it. They don't find their reward in getting work done in general, it has to be someone *else's* work, because that means somebody needs the Savior. Others will take advantage of them because they know the Savior will always be there.

37

Getting Over The Savior Complex

Once you recognize you have a savior complex, you're already heading in a good direction. The hardest part of change is acknowledging that you need to change. To get over a savior complex, you have to change ingrained habits and ingrained thinking. Here are some good ways to change your behavior on a daily basis:

- When your partner is talking about a problem they have, try to just listen and not offer to take over for them. If they ask you for help, say, "Well, what do *you* think you should do?"

- When your partner tells you about advice they were given by someone else, do not override it with your own thoughts.

- Let your partner go out with friends on their own and have interests apart from you, without making them feel guilty about it.

- Spend time away from your partner developing your own interests and friendships. This will help you form an identity that isn't based around "saving" your partner.

- If your partner makes a decision you don't think is right, try not to say anything. Let them make mistakes.

- Be happy for your partner when they accomplish something on their own, instead of disappointed or bitter that you weren't directly involved with that success. Be happy because they're happy.

The savior complex is deeply-rooted in how you see yourself and where you get your sense of worth. Getting to the heart of your beliefs is best done with a therapist who can act as a guide through your past. Here are some of the biggest issues you'll be considering:

- Why do you feel the need to "save" your partner? Is it because you only feel valuable when you serve a specific purpose?

- Make a list of your role models. Why do you admire them? Do they all look like saviors and white knights?

- Learn to become comfortable with yourself when you aren't playing a hero role. Think about all the things that define you and see how they make you a whole, worthy person.

- Think about how you see your partner - do you see them as an adult who is capable of their decisions, or someone who is helpless and needs constant guidance?

- Do you see your partner as someone who is trustworthy, or as someone who would always make the wrong decisions if you weren't around?

Chapter 6: The Coach

Codependents with a coach complex are similar to the Savior, but instead of seeing themselves as a hero, they see themselves as someone with the best advice. Instead of taking over things for their partner, they'll try to control situations by telling their partner what to do. Why do they do this? It's because Coaches live vicariously through their partners. If the Coach wishes they could get a promotion at work, they'll pressure their partner to get a promotion. Out of fear and insecurity, Coaches are unable to take responsibility for themselves, so they shift the focus to their partner. They believe if they can get their partner to change, everything will be great. Coaches want their partner's lives to look exactly like the life the Coach wants for themselves. They see themselves as a mirror reflection, not an independent person.

Coaches are control freaks. They're always on their partner with a "Do this, do that" mantra. Whenever their partner talks, the Coach is there to offer advice, play-by-plays, and "What you should have done is…" It becomes exhausting for the partner, who feels like they can't do anything right. The Coach feels like their partner is ignoring or dismissing them. Bitterness builds between the couple.

The End of Codependency

Here are some common traits displayed by a codependent with a coach complex:

- You always find fault in what your partner is doing or how they're acting.

- You spend all your time thinking about what your partner can do to improve themselves, and none thinking about yourself.

- When you're out with your partner, you're always watching them like a hawk and taking mental notes about things that bother you. When you get home, you break out the criticisms and go through the evening like an instant replay.

- You become very anxious when your partner doesn't follow your advice. You spend all day agonizing over what could go wrong and experience panic attacks.

- You use fear and the worst-case scenario to convince your partner to take your advice.

- You believe you give better advice than anyone else in your partner's life, and feel resentful when they listen to someone other than you.

- When your partner is telling a story, you're always interrupting to tell them what you think they should have done or said.

The End of Codependency

Coaching Your Friends And People At Work

Being friends with a Coach is difficult. The Coach is nosy
and always has an opinion about what's going on in their
friends' lives. They spend a lot of time thinking about what
their friends should do about every problem, and then lay it
all out before them. When the friends don't listen, the
Coach becomes irritated, even angry. People don't like to
spend time with others who are always telling them what to
do, so Coaches are often left out of gatherings or purposely
not told about problems going on their friends' lives. It can
be lonely.

Working with a Coach can be a mixed bag. Sometimes it
can be a good thing, because Coaches are always willing to
offer advice on a project and are usually very involved.
However, when the advice isn't wanted, a Coach's
colleagues quickly get annoyed. It can also be a problem
when a Coach tries to tell their boss what they should be
doing better. People will tell the Coach to just keep their
eyes on their own work, but a Coach has to have their
fingers in everything to feel valued. When their advice isn't
acted on, a Coach will feel unappreciated and anxious.

The End of Codependency

How To Fire The Coach Complex

Getting rid of your coach complex is all about keeping your mouth shut and quieting your mind. It isn't enough to just not give advice - there will be a lot of anxiety surrounding your obsession with what and how your partner is doing. Here are some ways to fire your inner coach:

- When you're with your partner, make it a rule to not offer any advice.

- When your partner talks, focus on just listening, and not analyzing their every move.

- If your partner asks for advice, turn it back around and ask them what *they* think would be best.

- If you see your partner doing something you don't like, don't say anything. To prevent hoarding that negative emotion, write it down in a journal and then counter it with something you really love about your partner.

- Give your partner at least one compliment a day.

- Your partner will do things that you don't agree with. Instead of obsessing over the problem, take

45

that time to deal with your anxiety.

- When your partner admits they made a mistake, do not say, "I told you so."

The next part of recovery really focuses on your long-held beliefs about yourself. Codependent Coaches feel a need to change their partners because they don't know how to change, or don't want to change, themselves. It can be scary to dig deep into your own mind for the first time, but it's necessary in order to make sure the Coach doesn't come right back. Therapy would be a very useful tool.

- Think about what specific things you want your partner to change and why. Are they things you also dislike about yourself?

- Criticisms are almost always rooted in some deeper fear. What fears are your concerns rooted in? For example, you perceive your partner's friendliness as flirtiness, and you're always telling them how to behave. This criticism is rooted in a lack of trust.

- When your partner doesn't take your advice, spend some time thinking about how you feel. Do you feel fear? A sense of emptiness or uselessness?

- Think about the kinds of emotions you feel when your partner fails. Do *you* feel like a failure when that happens?

- Focus on dealing with your anxiety. When you begin to stop coaching your partner, the anxiety will most likely be pretty bad at first. Ask a qualified therapist about how to deal with anxiety and research treatment techniques.

- Take more ownership over your life. If you want something, make it a goal to go after it yourself instead of pushing your partner towards it. As a specific example, if you want live a more active lifestyle, start taking walks by yourself instead of forcing your partner to join a gym.

Chapter 7: The People-Pleaser

On the surface, People-Pleasers just want everyone to be happy. However, People-Pleasers don't believe they're worthy of love unless others love them. To get that love, a People-Pleaser will do everything they can to make people like them. While an independent, empowered person believes they are inherently worthy of love, a People-Pleaser feels that they must earn it by being a social chameleon and changing into whoever the person they're with would like best. With their significant other, a People-Pleaser will put on a happy mask and work very hard to always be what they believe their partner wants, be it "The Breadwinner," "The Domestic Goddess," or "The Pillar of Strength." They'll say "yes" to everything and always defer to their partner's desires because they believe that will make them lovable.

The consequences of being a People-Pleaser are quick and painful. A People-Pleaser is immediately at risk for becoming a doormat to their partner, and if their partner is abusive in any way, the People-Pleaser's life will be miserable. Always prioritizing their partner's needs instead of their own can cause a lot of pain for the People-Pleaser. They won't be able to talk about it with their partner, because a People-Pleaser hates discussing negative emotions, believing it will make their partner stop loving them.

The End of Codependency

Even if their significant other isn't abusive, it will be hard for them to respect a People-Pleaser, because they'll start to see the People-Pleaser as spineless. They'll get frustrated when the codependent won't be able to make a decision without them, or talk about anything that might be controversial or reveal a difference of opinion. Basically, the partner of a People-Pleaser may get bored with the relationship.

Read on for some signs that you might be a People-Pleaser in your relationship:

- You always go to great lengths to meet your partner's every desire, including canceling plans with other people to do what your partner wants, neglecting work and other hobbies, doing something sexual that makes you uncomfortable, and so on.

- You never say "no," but you feel guilty when you even consider saying no to your partner.

- You're always anxious and apologizing just in case you might have done or said something your partner didn't like.

The End of Codependency

- You don't feel good about yourself unless your partner is happy with you and giving you compliments, affection, etc.

- You avoid confrontation and have developed systems for skirting around hard topics like finances, politics, and so on.

- When you feel sad, upset, or any other emotion that you feel your partner won't want to see, you shove it down and hide from your partner.

- You put every decision through the "Will this make my partner happy?" filter.

Being The Pleaser With Friends and Coworkers

People-pleasers are very closed off with everyone, including their friends. They tend to not share anything deep about themselves, because they're afraid others won't like what's inside. They'll hide all of their personal struggles, personality traits, and opinions. Relationships with People-Pleasers tend to not go below the surface because of this, meaning even though People-Pleasers *know* a lot of people, they don't have any true friends of the heart. Additionally, People-Pleasers get manipulated and taken advantage of a lot. Their friends get used to always having the People-Pleaser say "yes" to everything, so whenever they need a favor, they know exactly where to go.

At work, a People-Pleaser can get stressed out a lot. They're always taking on extra work, working really hard, and being taken for granted. They tend to bite off more than they can chew just because someone asked for help. Their own work can suffer because they're trying to juggle everybody else's jobs, too. When it comes to the tough decisions, the People-Pleaser often becomes paralyzed with anxiety knowing that they can't possibly make everybody happy. This can be a big problem when there's deadlines approaching and the boss is breathing down their neck.

Saying "No" to People-Pleasing

Once a person realizes they are lovable and don't have to earn that from anyone, they are free. If you're a People-Pleaser, learning to say "no" and loving yourself are key steps to escaping the codependency of people-pleasing. Your partner's attention and affection doesn't make you lovable - you are lovable on your own. Here are some concrete steps you can take to learn that:

- When your partner asks for a favor, say that you need to think about it. This allows you to think about whether or not it's a good idea to say yes.

- When you're meeting your partner for lunch on your break or you have another commitment coming up, set a time limit, so your partner doesn't monopolize your time.

- Don't give a series of excuses for or apologize for why you can't do something your partner wants. They should respect your decision regardless of the reason.

- Make a list about what you really don't like doing with (or for) your partner versus what you actually do enjoy. Get in touch with your feelings, so you

52

can start having a mind of your own and figuring out what your desires and needs are.

- Start saying "no" to the things on your dislike list, so you can still say "yes" to the things you yourself enjoy.

- When a topic of conversation comes up that usually makes you uncomfortable, be open with your partner about your fears, but don't run away from it. *(Note: If your partner is abusive and you avoid topics so you don't get hurt, apply this step to your therapist, friends, family, etc, so they can help you).*

- Try to do three things just for you every day.

Coming out of a people-pleasing mindset involves rewiring long-held beliefs about yourself. This may require going to therapy alone and spending time focusing on your own dreams and desires. Here are some thought exercises that can help:

- When you do something just for you, take a moment to analyze your feelings. If you feel guilt, use positive affirmation to tell yourself that it's

53

okay to take care of yourself and your needs.

- Visit a therapist who can help you dig up why you feel selfish and bad when you aren't taking care of someone else's needs.

- If you haven't been in touch with your own feelings and desires in a long time, spend time alone figuring out what you really want out of life and your relationship.

- Work on learning that confrontation and hard conversations are all a part of building a strong, healthy relationship.

- Begin living through a filter of "I should treat myself as lovingly and kindly as I treat others."

- Focus on self-acceptance, self-empowerment, and self-love with the mentality that you cannot give the best of yourself to others unless you are a whole person. This can help you get an idea of the bigger picture and what's at stake for your relationship.

The End of Codependency

Chapter 8: What If Your Partner Is The Codependent One?

What should you do if you realize that your partner is codependent? This is a really tricky position to be in. If you recognize that you have an addiction/untreated mental illness, and have been allowing your partner to be codependent, the only thing you can do is take responsibility for yourself. Go seek treatment and encourage your partner to start therapy aimed towards codependents.

You might not have any kind of addiction or "classic" trait that creates a codependent, which makes dealing with your partner's codependency even trickier. The first thing you need to realize is that you can't "fix" the codependency. The root of the problem lies in your partner's lack of self-esteem and lack of self-love. No matter how much you love them, you can't cure them. You might even begin to become codependent yourself and take on the role of a Savior.

So, what *can* you do? Essentially, the only thing you can change is your own reactions to codependent behavior. This will disrupt your partner's usual habits and guide them

56

towards a new behavior system, hopefully one that isn't based on codependency.

Responding To The Martyr

Depending on the kind of codependent your partner is, they will behave differently. If
they are a martyr, they will baby you, sulk, and complain to everyone but you. A good response to this kind of behavior would be to not allow them to treat you like a child. As mentioned before, taking responsibility for your life. Don't let your partner do things for you that you can do yourself, especially when you haven't asked for help. This prevents them from collecting a laundry list of things they do for you and feeling sorry for themselves.

When they sulk, try to talk to them about their feelings. This will make them uncomfortable, but showing them that you care about *their* feelings is good. It also forces them to talk to *you* instead of family and friends who affirm their victimhood. They won't be able to suffer in silence any longer if you're building a bridge to better communication.

Responding To The Savior

For the Savior codependent, show your partner that you don't need to be saved. Do things for yourself, handle your own problems, and fight your own battles. You might have to spend some time thinking about everything that your partner does for you, because having the Savior take care of everything has become part of your routine. If you really do feel like you need help, just turn to someone else in your life who isn't a Savior.

Not turning to your partner for a rescue will throw your partner for a loop, because they get their purpose from saving you, so expect conflict. You will have to talk it out, possibly in therapy, so your partner can begin to learn that they are valuable and lovable outside of that white knight role. Show them attention and appreciation when they aren't behaving like a Savior, so they know you still love them. Invite them to share in the successes where they weren't involved. This will make them feel less isolated when you are able to accomplish things on your own. Again, however, a Savior needs to see their codependency as a problem in order to change.

Responding To The Coach

When you're the partner of a Coach, they will constantly be telling you what to do. You probably feel like you're constantly being evaluated. The only way to respond to this kind of codependency is to stay strong. Be content with who you are, even when your partner points out things they dislike. Just by being comfortable in your own skin, you're being a good example for your partner. If you do have flaws that you want to improve on (i.e. drinking too much, lying, yelling, etc), take responsibility.

For your part, show your partner that you are trustworthy and that you are capable of making good decisions. If you have a history of poor judgment, you will need to prove yourself. Even when you have become more attentive to your actions, your partner will likely still offer advice at every turn and become anxious when you don't listen. However, at least you have facts on your side when you let them know that you *are* capable. Don't get angry at them when they're coaching you. That won't help.

Responding To The People-Pleaser

With a People-Pleaser, you can encourage their independence without directly instructing them, which would just further enable the codependency. Instead, don't let them just go along with whatever you want to do or your opinions. Ask them what they think. Show them that you really do value what they have to say. Ask them what they would like to do, and don't let them default to, "Whatever you want." Think hard about asking your partner for favors; if you can do it yourself or have someone else do it, do that. You don't want to continue affirming your partner's People-Pleaser role.

Most importantly, when your partner is vulnerable, do *not* judge them. If they believe that you dislike something about them, they will withdraw back into their people-pleasing, having had their beliefs confirmed. Celebrate every part of your partner, especially those parts that they try to hide. Exercise forgiveness freely and learn how to disagree in a calm, loving way.

Chapter 9: How To Love Yourself

Past chapters have discussed how gaining self-esteem and learning to love yourself is key to overcoming every kind of codependency, so it's worth covering more methods more thoroughly. Anyone who has struggled with low self-esteem can benefit from these techniques, but for people with codependent behaviors, it is especially important. There are three "categories" of techniques: thought training, tangible actions, and habit elimination.

Thought training is all about setting goals, changing your perceptions, and committing to the journey. This makes up the base for the other techniques, and are principles you will constantly return to. No one ever really "masters" these; they'll always be at the back of your mind. Tangible actions are the concrete steps you take to build self-esteem. This book has already listed actions that each type of codependent can do, but there are always more that are useful. Habit elimination is often the trickiest part of learning to love yourself, because it's much harder to break a habit than to add a new one to your routine, but it's just as important. Let's get started:

Thought Training

- **Be honest with yourself**

The first step to change is realizing that you actually need
to change. Be honest with yourself about your life and your
codependency. Ask yourself the hard questions, like, "Am I
happy in this relationship?" "Do I love myself?" and "Am I
willing to focus on my own needs?" Starting to be open
with yourself trains you to be vulnerable, which is
something you will have to be with your partner in order to
achieve happiness. Asking tough questions also trains your
mind to really focus inward and figure out your desires.

- **Start paying attention to your daily thoughts**

It's easy to just live your life on automatic, without paying
attention to what's going on inside your head. In order to
break free from codependency, you have to start listening
to your inner voices, or, the thoughts that follow you
throughout the day. Are your thoughts mostly negative and
telling you that you aren't lovable? Are they fearful? By
paying closer attention to your thoughts throughout the
day, you are gaining insight into what makes you tick and
why you act the way you do. Once you identify the tone of
the thoughts that make up your day, you can start to unravel
their effect on your actions.

● **Commit to forgiving yourself**

This process isn't going to be easy. You will have relapses and times when you want to give up. Right now, commit to being merciful with yourself. Forgive yourself for every bad decision you've made in the past and every bad decision you'll make in the future. Self-loathing is based in the refusal to forgive, so by letting go of the need to judge and condemn yourself, you're on the road to healing.

Tangible Actions

- **Keep a journal**

Taking a little time every day to journal is a fantastic way to get in touch with your feelings. At the beginning of each day, write down at least one thing that you like about yourself. Imagine that you're facing yourself, and have to come up with a compliment. What would you say if you were a totally separate person? This can help you treat yourself with kindness. Write down your goals and dreams, fears and anxieties, as well.

- **Try self-affirmation mantras**

These are like gold nuggets of positivity that counter any negative thoughts that pop up during the day. You can even write them down and carry around index cards, so if you find yourself slipping into self-loathing, pull a card out and read it to yourself. Buy a whiteboard and write down quotes, so the first thing you see in the morning is something positive. You can also start a quote book of your favorite sayings and spend time reading through them all.

- **Do things that are good for your body**

Your physical health is closely-connected to your mental state, so taking care of your body will make a big impact on your mind. Adjust your diet so you're eating lots of fresh food, like vegetables, fruit, lean proteins, and drinking water. If you haven't been to the doctor in a while, schedule a check-up. If you don't exercise, start walking or doing yoga. You can take on more ambitious physical activity if you want, just make sure that it doesn't turn into another source of stress and guilt for you.

● **Have fun**

Codependents have very stressful lives, so just having fun and relaxing can work wonders. Spend time with people who make you laugh. There really aren't any rules; just do what sets you at ease and doesn't bring you stress.

● **Get help**

Depending on how severe your codependency is, the best tangible action you can take is to get help. This means therapy. A good therapist will never judge you, they'll help you set goals, and you'll feel comfortable sharing anything with them. Sometimes it takes a little while to find the therapist that's right for you, but it's totally worth it.

Habit Elimination

- **Cut out toxic people**

What friends or family are always reaffirming negative thoughts you have about yourself? They gotta go. It's simpler (though not necessarily easier) to cut out toxic friends than family, so if you have family members who always put you down, commit to spending less time with them. You don't have to give excuses or explain yourself. If they try to guilt you into spending time with them, stay strong. Replace the time you would spend with them doing healthy, self-esteem building activities.

- **Cut out self-destructive coping techniques**

What have you always done to cope with negative feelings? Do you drink? Eat? Sulk? Complain about yourself and your partner to friends? That needs to stop in order for you to move forward. Breaking a habit is hard, but replacing it with a better coping technique like the tangible actions can make it a lot easier.

Chapter 10: What Does A Healthy Relationship Look Like?

What does a healthy relationship look like? For many codependent people, they've never really had a truly healthy relationship, so they don't even know what to look for. Here are the essentials:

Good Communication

When a couple has good communication skills, there is no fear. You can express your feelings without fear of emotional or physical violence. You can even disagree and fight, without fearing that your partner will play dirty or stop loving you. Both members of the relationship are able to clearly and directly express their feelings, and don't avoid the tough conversations. Of course, even healthy relationships aren't perfect, and communication can't always be good, but it's definitely more positive than negative.

Trust

Trust is the building block of a good relationship. When you trust your partner, you are comfortable with them having their own life. You don't worry about infidelity or lies. When they tell you where they're going, you believe them. You are secure about their love and commitment to you, their handling of finances, and all the other "big life stuff."

Respect

Respect and trust go hand-in-hand. You can't trust someone unless you respect them, and you can't respect someone unless you trust them. When there's respect in your relationship, you make important decisions together. Neither one of you is constantly questioning the other, because you respect their choices. You take advice from your partner, and vice versa, because you both value the other's opinions. The other crucial part about respect is that there's respect about boundaries, be it sexual, emotional, what have you.

Self-care

In a healthy relationship, both members practice good self-care. You understand that being healthy on your own is a crucial part of having a healthy relationship. You love yourself, have confidence, and are able to take time to focus on you, without being sabotaged by self-guilt. Self-care involves both physical, mental, and spiritual needs. Go to the doctor. Take mental health days. Take prescribed medications. Eat healthy. Exercise. Pray. Lie in the sun like a cat. Whatever fuels you and gives you rest, that's self-care.

Honesty/Vulnerability

Like good communication, being honest and vulnerable with your partner comes without fear. You never feel threatened or afraid to speak your mind with your partner, even when you are disagreeing about something. You're able to share secrets, admit mistakes, and have tough conversations without fear of violence or emotional manipulation. You're also able to be yourself - warts and all - without feeling judged. Your partner should love you for *you,* all of you, and not for a mask you put on that hides all the embarrassing and dark parts. Healthy couples know the worst things about each other, and still love one another.

Forgiveness

Forgiveness is crucial in a relationship. No one is perfect, and both you and your partner will make mistakes and hurt each other. Instead of harboring grudges and resentment, a strong couple will exercise mercy and forgiveness. This isn't the same as letting your partner "get away" with something. There's genuine regret and genuine grace. When a partner apologizes to the other for a mistake, they are making a commitment to not repeating that mistake. When a partner says, "I forgive you," they are committing to not holding that mistake over their partner as emotional blackmail.

Time Apart

A healthy couple is able to spend time apart. In fact, time apart is a critical part of the relationship. Each individual has their own life, friends, and hobbies. When you're apart, you miss each other, but neither of you are at a loss. You aren't constantly checking in with your partner, stressing about what their doing, or just wandering around the house waiting for your loved one to return. You're both actually able to use the time apart to really focus on your own desires and needs, and recharge. This makes the relationship stronger and healthier.

Support

You have dreams and goals. So does your partner. You both support each other and truly want the other to be happy and fulfilled. Whether this means moving for a job, taking over chores, or just being there with a hot cup of coffee late at night, you're always there for each other. You don't feel like you need to downplay your successes, or like you're in a competition with each other. If one of you makes more money than the other, you see it as a shared success, not an invitation for rivalry or resentment. On the other side of support, there should be gratitude and appreciation. Being supportive of a partner frequently requires sacrifices, and the partner who made the sacrifice should feel like their loved one truly appreciates it, and isn't ever dismissive.

Fun

Never underestimate the importance of fun. A couple in a good relationship is able to have a blast with each other. Whether it's just hanging out at home or going out, a happy couple will enjoy being in each other's company. You make each other laugh and always feel comfortable in each other's presence. Sex is not a source of stress or danger, and you can be lighthearted and goofy.

Conclusion

Codependency robs a person of their individuality. It poisons relationships, enables abuse, and fuels unhappiness. Codependent tendencies are usually born in a person's childhood, and those from dysfunctional households are most at risk for becoming codependent adults. However, everyone can become codependent. Unfortunately, codependency is often romanticized in the media, and people are told that true love *should* be all-consuming and possessive. This just isn't true. Codependency breeds chronic insecurity, anxiety, depression, and even physical ailments like high blood pressure and digestive problems.

This book described four types of codependents: the Martyr, the Savior, the Coach, and the People-Pleaser. Each type displays distinct traits like continuing to suffer without thinking of solutions (the Martyr), becoming jealous a partner takes advice from someone else (the Savior), constant criticism (the Coach), and being unable to say no to anything (the People-Pleaser), but all four types are based in a lack of self-esteem. A codependent does not love themselves, so they depend on their partner to define them. For the other member in the relationship, responding to

78

The End of Codependency

codependency can be very difficult. It isn't possible to force another person to change, but the partner of a codependent can take steps to help, such as not allowing the codependent to "baby" them, encouraging the codependent to express their own opinion, and so on. However, the key to change can only come from the codependent.

Building self-esteem is imperative to breaking free from codependency. This book has provided with an arsenal of techniques, both practical and thought-based. By seeking therapy, paying attention to your thoughts, and avoiding people who reaffirm negative beliefs, you are well on your way to truly loving yourself. You are worthy. You are valuable. It's time to start believing.

Manufactured by Amazon.ca
Bolton, ON

12480020R00046